Every Syllable Begins a Universe
Rogue Linguistics Vol. 1

Every Syllable Begins a Universe
Rogue Linguistics Vol. 1

Kimo RedeR

☙❧
☙❧
Winged Sandal Press
Dobbs Ferry, New York

Every Syllable Begins a Universe
(Rogue Linguistics Vol. 1)
Copyright © 2024 by John Reder

[paperback]

ISBN: 979-8-218-53817-0

Design/Layout/Editing: Twink Reder

The front cover art is an ancient Tibetan painting of the Kalachakra syllables, a Ring of Wisdom mandala in the Tantric tradition.

The back cover art is a colorized woodblock print of a Mayan king dictating to his court scribe.

Manufactured in the U.S.A.

Winged Sandal Press
Dobbs Ferry, New York

This book is dedicated to the birdsong of New York's Hudson Valley, whose warbles, chirrups, trills, quavers, screeches, caws, twitters, and hoots create universes of their own.

WSP

Only a few words—like "letter" and "syllable" and "ink"— can point directly to things inside of themselves as well as outside of themselves. More than a few verbs seem to want a "stalling tense" in between their present and future tenses and a "prolonging tense" in between their past and present tenses.

      The word "silence," to be ultimately true to itself,
             would need to be composed of
          the unpronounced s in "apropos"
                    i in "abstain"
                     l in "calm"
                  e in "unnamed"
                  n in "solemn"
              c in "quiescent"
             and e in "space."

≈∞≈∞≈∞≈∞≈∞≈∞≈∞≈∞≈∞≈∞≈∞≈∞≈∞≈∞≈∞≈

If one lost one's premolars with the use of one's first curse-word but gained postmolars at the use of one's last curse-word, the dental profession and the dictionary profession would take interrelated notice.

Lips closed with duct tape by abductors
      tend to transfer their elocution to the eyebrows
          but eyebrows plucked into near-silence
don't always transfer what they can't articulate downward.

A typist doesn't need a piano-player's page-turner because of the spacing-bar and the "scroll" function just as surely as a piano-player's black keys don't concern themselves with toner refills.

Is a split personality with a French accent in one persona and a Spanish accent in another briefly Basque or liminally Latin during its switchovers?

∞∞∞∞∞∞∞∞∞∞∞∞∞∞∞∞∞∞∞∞∞∞∞∞∞∞∞∞∞∞∞∞∞

An antonym alert can't be unrung by simply insisting that one's indecision can't tell an opposite from an auditory illusion. A synonym-siren can't be re-sounded by merely stating that one's sense of sameness splits every singularity into two similars.

Since an ambiguous piece of writing suffers from "iffiness," certain excessive grocery lists must surely suffer from "and-iness," and certain prolonging indecisions from "or-iness," and certain too-direct threats and insults from "at-iness."

Some threats are more fittingly written in lipstick than in eyeliner just as some promises are more fittingly erased by an electrolysis wand than by an exfoliating soap.

The word "staccato"'s trio of doubled letters
   taken as separate freeze-frames or notches on a branch
      plays out its meaning as a melody
         and its connotation as a cadence.

Whether to hyphenate "wallpaper" into "wall-paper" is a question of privacy retention. Whether to hyphenate "broadside" into "broad-side" is a question of publicity enhancement. Whether to hyphenate "blackbird" into "black-bird" is as ontological as it is ornithological.

An axiom is often a place
  where our intellect can put up its cerebral feet
    loosen its medullar belt-buckle,
interlace its verbal fingers behind its mental head
      and paddle a cognitive ukulele
         down a meandering rivulet called Reverie.

A squadron of ganged-up periods (…) means something less firm and more open-ended than a solitary period, in a reassuring example of strength-in-singularity.

The equilateral "and" connecting "so" and "so"
   can't lean more to one side than the other
      unlike the "and" connecting "to" and "fro"
         which has to learn to rock, swivel, and vacillate.

«±«±«±«±«±«±«±«±«±«±«±«±«±«±«±«±«±«

In terms of suitable vowel-containment, the long double "e" in the midst of "between" is presumably more comfortable in its host word than the counterintuitively prolonged double "o" in "soon."

In a more polymorphous world,
    not only would "oracles" come to us via the ear,
        but "optacles" via the eye
            and "nasacles" via the nose
                and "tactacles" via the skin.

We have "foothold" and "toehold" and "handhold" in our vocabulary but not "backhold" or "kneehold" or "hiphold" because not many people are familiar with the practical needs of sheer-face mountain climbing.

When "carbon-copied" and "carbon-dated" collide
    an object feels imitated and antiquated at once
      but when a promise and a plea decide to pistol-duel
        at an agreed-on number of paces
    a paradox can no longer patrol its own perimeter.

If letters behaved like (or were categorized like) numbers, what would an "irrational letter" be? Are vowels arguably more irrational than consonants because they are more amorphous and guttural and less firmly contoured by the lips?

A sibilant spelling-bee held in sub-sub-zero conditions causes words like "Sahara" and "savannah" to be stuttered on more often than more seasonable words.

Sometimes the state capital of a mission statement grows so semantically uncentered it becomes its own suburb. Sometimes the state government of a declarative statement is so self-correcting it ends up segregated from any semblance of sincerity.

Which syllable of the word "procrastinate" contains the bulb-housing for its pause signal depends on which syllable of the word "terminate" contains its brake-light.

≳ȧ≳ȧ≳ȧ≳ȧ≳ȧ≳ȧ≳ȧ≳ȧ≳ȧ≳ȧ≳ȧ≳ȧ≳ȧ≳ȧ≳ȧ

The butt-end of a pen swings and thrusts like a conductor's baton during the act of writing. The string section of said pen are the sinews and tendons that guide its ball-pointed glide. The tympani section is a tapping on a desktop to punctuate periods of indecision.

In a game of semiotic solitaire, the word "inferno" erased with a firehose trumps the word "dessert" written with a baker's icing-nozzle, trumps the word "waver" spoken into a wind-tunnel.

If a proper surname being converted into a progressive verb is a sign of historical impact, Maoing and Stalining are probably further along in their application process than Nixoning or Clintoning are in their bids for common usage but also further along toward the prospect of being toppled like a statue in a public square.

One can imagine a voice-recognition apparatus
   so sensitive and hair-triggered and medically alert
      it could translate all our coughs, snorts, and wheezes
         into dictionary-approved words and phrases
            that describe respiratory exasperation.

The sentence "You and I disagree." is itself a quadripartisan grammar-agreement. The sentence "I am out for myself" is a metronome that likes to loiter at both ends of its swing.

In our optic vocabulary, we can "stare daggers"
   and so we should also be figuratively able
      to wink portholes and windows
         and glance small, fleeting shards of broken glass
and rub a mirror clean with a self-irritated roll of our eyes.

Sometimes the premature turning of a page can reduce a potboiler to room temperature and push a cliffhanger into a plummet and embalm a murder mystery into immortality.

According to a law of self-echoing suffixes, a luxury apartment that is not fully up to its claims is "lavish-ish" and garbage not quite ready to be disposed is "rubbish-ish" and a resin that doesn't cause wood to shine is only "varnish-ish."

☼ ◇ ☼◇ ☼◇ ☼◇ ☼◇ ☼◇ ☼◇ ☼◇ ☼

If every one of the ten Mosaic commandments were carved separately on a tablet made of a different kind of substance, the prohibition against graven images would have to remain unillustrated and the warning against stealing would need to be placed on a non-precious stone unlikely to induce coveting and the decree against false witness would be placed on a stone impossible to counterfeit.

The first typewriters used a foot-lever somewhere in between a sewing-machine's foot pedal and a piano's sustain pedal and was manufactured by a gun-maker, thus bridging the gaps between caliber and concerto and costume-making.

Sometimes a Castilian's rolled r's can resemble a spiral staircase inlaid with Moorish marble. Sometimes the gleaming peak of an Arabic guttural can erect a figurative minaret out of its upwelling air. Sometimes an English accent snaps upward on every syllable like drawbridges being pulled up around a castle's moat.

The prefix "dis-" taken from "dismemberment"
          has been amputated
    as surely as the prefix "de-" taken from "deport"
          has been exiled
    and the prefix "mis"- taken from "miscalculate"
          has been subtracted.

$$\S\infty\S\infty\S\infty\S\infty\S\infty\S\infty\S\infty\S\infty\S\infty\S\infty\S\infty\S\infty\S\infty\S$$

A similar spelling/significance irony
        places "and" inside of "meander,"
        "but" inside of "rebuttal,"
            and "or" inside of "coordinate."

Chinese pictograms are made of "radicals" instead of "liberals" for the purpose of the "conservation"-of-language. The three separate Chinese characters for "woman," "door," and "tree" add up to the character for "forest" like a superimposed chord genderizing, inviting entrance, and resonating like a solid plank of wood all at once.

When composing a memoir, a pen is like a buffing pad trying to polish a blank page into a rear-view mirror. When composing a prophecy, a pen is like a periscope trying to levitate and see above its past-and-present-tense static interference.

If our word-processors once dwelled in a simpler Gutenberg Galaxy, they now also inhabit a Nano-science Nebula, a Simulacra Supernova, a Post-History Pulsar, a Dark Matter Data-Overload, and an Event-Planner Event Horizon.

ᗢᶘᕲᶘᗢᶘᕲᶘᗢᶘᕲᶘᗢᶘᕲᶘᗢᶘᕲᶘᗢᶘᕲᶘᗢᶘᕲ

The "plays" in a fishing line and a line of poetry are both matters of tension, tug, and tautness. The criss-crossing patterns of a fishing net and the suspense plot of a detective novel are both matters of casting, current-flow, and capture.

From "rival" to "opponent" to "nemesis"
   is a series of semantic upgrades
      like a stone skipped across a pond called Escalation
         or ever-ascending, ever-resonating rungs
      on a Ladder of No Return
   even though the "us" in "consensus" is more at home
than the "we" in "weapon" or the "our" in "tournament."

A stone etched with the word "silence" held under the tongue is usually self-fulfilling. A stone etched with the word "swallow" held on the tip of the tongue is generally self-daring. A stone etched with the word "scream" is eventually self-expelling.

The molecular bond between syllables is weaker
    than the atomic bond between letters
but stronger than the hormonal bond between sentences.

    A language that places its adverbs in front of its verbs may be too eager to reveal its motives. A language that places its adjectives behind its nouns may be too reluctant to expose its evaluations. A language that glues its modifiers directly onto the words they describe may be all-too-willing to reflect the quantum blur between objects, attributes, and actions.

    Kafka famously believed a book should be a pick-axe
      on a reader's frozen inner ocean
    without allowing that certain books operate more
      like a mallet on a loose floorboard
        or a staple-gun on the fluttering roof-shingle
    of our inner summer bungalow.

The possessive apostrophe that allows one noun to take ownership of another is more imperious than the contracting apostrophe that allows "cannot" and "does not" to relax their posture and less additive than the apostrophe that forms the plurals of numbers and letters.

Some words appeal to our naked eye and naked ear equally, but some induce eye-strain even before they fall out of earshot, and some offer an eyewitness and an earwitness able to overrule each other.

Some memos are so inter-office they have carpet burns across their consonants and water-coolers welling up inside their vowels. Some interoffice memos imply an extended index finger that means "Take notice" when it is immobile and "Too late for noticing" when it is mobilized into a wag.

The cultivated Oxford stammer of England's hyper-educated classes is a relief-map of all the conversational byroads not taken and all of the acts of Empire unremarked-on. The hard-bitten staccato of a caffeinated Wall St. stammer sometimes trails off like a banking PIN trying to remember its own final digit.

When "versa" runs out ahead of "vice" as proof that "vice versa" can submit to its own prescription, the "quid" and the "quo" in "quid pro quo" try to figure out a way to appear simultaneously (instead of one after the other) in a sentence.

    The ceasefire between "perhaps" and "maybe"
        models its own negotiations
          on the acrimony-avoiding divorce agreement
            between "therefore" and "hence"
        and the steely-nerved custody battle
          between "moreover" and "additionally."

On the chessboard of grammar, certain adjectives are allowed more diagonal maneuvers and longer hesitations than others. On the checkerboard of grammar, our past-tense verbs aren't yet sub-classified into checkered-past, forgotten-past, or full-circle-past varieties.

    In excessively sibilant terms
        the static in between our semantic stations
           is a snowstorm trying to sniff itself
                and a sneeze snorted up silence's sinus cavity.

A lipogram is a literary work in which a particular letter is selected *not* to appear, offering a steep challenge to a history of Saudi Arabia without a *q* or a history of brand names without an *x*.

Sometimes a confession is so selectively self-edited it turns into a boast. Sometimes a drop-crate full of adjectives needs to be parachuted into a sentence that is unable to otherwise illustrate itself.

《±

Climbing up a sentence's ladder, the rungs marked "consonant" tend to creak where the rungs marked "vowel" tend to groan. Sliding down a sentence's ladder, the rungs marked "punctuation" tend to remain silent and deferential.

In an adjusted grammar in which nouns as well as verbs have tenses:
 "soil" is the past tense of "floor"
 and "build" is the future tense of "blueprint,"
 "beard" is both the past and the future tense of "razor"
 and "coincidence" is the concurrent tense
 of "happenstance."

If our own speech were visible (as cartoon caption-bubbles) as well as audible to us, our sense of agency (and impact) would be as inflated as only a bubble can be.

A word is not a gauge to measure an object's correspondence to it, nor an object a touchstone to measure a word's tactile sense, nor a word's objective case a way to make its meaning less subjective.

Around the Profanity Zodiac, which words wear horns and which words wear fins is determined by which words hold scales and which words launch arrows. Around the Deception Zodiac, being lied-to isn't as bad as being lied-at, just as being lied-around is generally more forgivable than being lied-about.

A truly flexible vow of silence would need a volume knob that could switch up and down from "hush" to "quietude," and from "lull" to "reticence," and undercut the woofer and top off the tweeter on a stereophonic urge to speak.

If our "horizon" is set by the limits of our perceptions, our "core-izon" is set by the limits of our self-inspection, our "door-izon" by our refusal to enter or depart, and our "floor-izon" by our unwillingness to recognize our foundations.

If a word that is all vowel or a sentence that is all verb is an invertebrate, then a word that is all consonant suffers from grammatical calcium deposits, as does a sentence that is all noun. If our taste-buds were a committee of language-legislators, some words would be so savory they would barely be semantic.

≷ả≷ả≷ả≷ả≷ả≷ả≷ả≷ả≷ả≷ả≷ả≷ả≷ả≷

In the Era of the Soundbite, the person who needs to verbally taste, chew, mull, and swallow is operating at a dietary and digestive disadvantage.

In terms of time-keeping idioms:
"moment to moment" is to Precarious
as "day to day" is to Pragmatic
and "year to year" is to Prospective.

If our stomach grew a new compartment every time we expressed hunger and our liver grew a new lobe every time we requested a drink, our vocabulary and our viscera would begin to grow on the same vine. If the Hippocratic Oath were held to a Herculean standard, our senses of "healing" and "hoisting" would need to be adjusted.

Sometimes there is an irony so great it can cause a set of "inverted commas" to perform a complete somersault. Sometimes a dictionary is a bank using its own grammar as its guard and its vocabulary as its vault and its linguistics as a loan officer.

↓ḋ↓ḋ↓ḋ↓ḋ↓ḋ↓ḋ↓ḋ↓ḋ↓ḋ↓ḋ↓ḋ↓ḋ↓ḋ↓ḋ↓

If a haiku written from bottom to top could more effectively portray an effusion of New Year's fireworks, a diagonally lined piece of paper would be needed to best describe a mudslide.

When libraries go up in flame
    their bibles burn a riot-squad blue,
        their sex manuals glow a carnal scarlet
            their interoffice memos smell of grey flannel,
and their coloring books red-line their own rainbows.

English has the largest vocabulary of any world language, but a heap of all of the items that English has no noun for would be taller than the Tower of Babel times ten.

Some of us are more hat-tip than nod when saying hello
      more checkmark than salute when saying goodbye
and more finger-cross than shrug when agreeing to linger.

☼◇☼◇☼◇☼◇☼◇☼◇☼◇☼◇☼

Sometimes a coinage is willing to emerge from the cocoon of its protective quotation marks and asks for diplomatic immunity in the front lobby of a dictionary. Sometimes a ten-syllable science term's prefix occupies a different ontological zip-code than its suffix.

If war is the human event that makes our vocabulary grow fastest, a ceasefire is a slowdown in semantic overdrive as well as a stoppage in mortal massacre.

Sometimes the maybe-men standing behind a yes-man are more perceptive, just as sometimes the perhaps-people behind a naysayer are more accurate.

Frequently, excessive Profanity is a tin cup
   used to bang on our vocabulary's jail-cell door
      or an idiomatic aerosol paint-can we use
      to blot out our conscience's security camera
      or a hell-bent tractor used to mow
   obscene-but-scenic circles in a field of swaying corn.

§∞§∞§∞§∞§∞§∞§∞§∞§∞§∞§∞§∞§∞§

The unused portion of an interrupted scolding cannot be refunded for future-feud stamps. The suicide note that sounds like an op-ed piece cannot straddle the generic boundaries of Despair and Demand.

If our consonants were required to write an annual reappointment request to continue their deployment, q and x and z would need to perform a more frenetic song and dance than the others.

The puncture-able word "balloon" can be spelled out of twisted coat-hangers more easily than the puncturing word "coat-hanger" can be spelled out of twisted balloons, but the scattering word "wind" can be written temporarily in sand more easily than easily-scattered word "sand" can be visibly suspended on the wind.

Rulers have to be rigid so centimeters can be stable just as scales have to be steady so ounces can be un-jostled and glossaries have to obey gravity so that our lexicon doesn't levitate.

ᗝʃ☊Ɜᗝʃ☊Ɜᗝʃ☊Ɜᗝʃ☊Ɜᗝʃ☊Ɜᗝʃ☊Ɜᗝʃ☊Ɜᗝʃ☊Ɜᗝʃ☊Ɜ

Sometimes the pause following a period is as personal as a private parking space. Sometimes the pause before a punchline is as unpaid as an appearance on public programming.

When a quotation overflows its self-bestowed banks,
    it moistens the floodplain of allusion
        irrigates the estuary of cross-reference
            and fertilizes the archipelago of urban legend.

An especially incoherent email deflected off a geo-stationary satellite hasn't yet caused our ozone layer to develop a criterion for grammar rays as well as gamma rays.

The two d's in "dud" argue
over which stands for Defective.
The two d's in "forbidding" wrangle
over which best embodies Danger.
The two d's in "puddle" feud
over which aspires to Deluge.

≈∞≈∞≈∞≈∞≈∞≈∞≈∞≈∞≈∞≈∞≈∞≈∞≈∞≈

Whether an undecided voter builds a wall of Moderately around his Maybe depends on whether he has erected a wall of Potentially around his Perhaps.

A transitive verb's tense-deciding suffix is a trailer-hitch, either ready to drag, dragging, or having dragged its direct object toward its grammatical Fate.

Sometimes a sentence has to decide if it is the "Caution" tape or the chalk outline around the contours of a mental event. Sometimes Irony Incarnate is deliberately meaning to mutter the adverb "accidentally" but uttering "on purpose" in error instead.

Irony embodied is a blank fortune cookie ribbon saying "Figure out your own Fate" or a twig-colored ribbon tied to a tree-trunk saying "Tell me apart from my terrain."

▨▨▨

In certain languages, an obituary is trained to avoid certain adjectives just as an advice column is trained to embrace certain euphemisms.

When a noun sidesteps its adjective a modifier-miss has occurred. When a verb outstares its adverb an action-arrogance has been inflicted. When a run-on sentence skips over its commas a syntactic steeplechase has been initiated.

When a misnomer and a malpropism play pantomime in front of a motion-sensor, a mangled proverb ensues. When the word "decline"'s own decline is steep enough it changes its name to "deadfall." When the word "uprising" grows intoxicated on its own ascent it changes its name to "insurrection."

The words "game" and "charades" performed in a game of charades both require a frantic pointing and gesturing inward. The word "arguably" seems more confident about sitting at the front of a sentence than the word "admittedly" because it is more of a conceit than a concession.

≈∞≈∞≈∞≈∞≈∞≈∞≈∞≈∞≈∞≈∞≈∞≈∞≈∞≈

When "like bringing coals to Newcastle" starts feeling lonely, introduce her to "like bringing bolt-flanges to Birmingham" and "like bringing heavy nitrogen to Hull" and "like bringing boat-builders to Bristol."

If one could learn advanced French via a week-long saline IV drip, one could absorb conversational German via a 24-hour dermal patch, and take in a trade-pidgin with a few sips from an eyedropper.

If languages had their own version of an unemployment rate, slang terms would hit Skid Row fairly often, deep-science jargons would write desperate grant proposals with one hand while operating a particle-collider with the other, and the words for numbers and primary colors would have guaranteed job insurance.

If our verbal grammar were an analogue clock half-past a dangling participle and quarter to a comma-splice, would both look forward to the eraser provided by an hour-hand.

《±《±《±《±《±《±《±《±《±《±《±《±《±《±《±《±

We refer to "typefaces" but not to "typeflanks" because we haven't yet mastered the art of reading from print's posterior side. Sometimes a hyphen is a forward slash fallen on its face, and sometimes it is an ellipsis coagulated into a solid line.

If broken Latin comes in pottery shards
    broken Japanese comes in mahogany splinters
        broken German comes in howitzer shrapnel
and broken Arabic comes in wind-blown sand-grains.

A phrase using "until" as an appetizer and "unless" as an aperitif is also inclined to use "although" as a palate-cleanser and "ultimately" as an after-dinner mint.

   Semantically, a sentence, like a scale,
   is only as symmetrical as its sides
   because a slide is only as slippery as its surface
   and a seesaw is only as suspended as its center-post.

⁂⁂⁂⁂⁂⁂⁂⁂⁂⁂⁂⁂⁂

In a perfectly executed compound-noun passive progression, bystander turns to bysitter to bystooper to byslumper to bysleeper. In an idiomatic state of equilibrium, the word "ink" when it is spoken is no more out of its element than the word "sound" when it is written.

Sometimes a revolutionary wields Perhaps like a bayonet because a pragmatist wears Conceivably like a raincoat, and a reactionary wears Maybe like a suit of armor.

As we learned during WW2, language is not a code, which is why Navajo cannot be "broken" but only slowly and organically "absorbed." As we learned from cinema studies, nearly half of a film is blank space in between its frames, and so a sentence is largely the sub-semantic hum in between its syllables.

The "the" before Bahamas, Philippines, and Congo is colonial where the "the" before Netherlands is honorific and the "the" before Bronx is pugnacious.

꠰ἀ꠰ἀ꠰ἀ꠰ἀ꠰ἀ꠰ἀ꠰ἀ꠰ἀ꠰ἀ꠰ἀ꠰ἀ꠰ἀ꠰ἀ꠰ἀ꠰ἀ

Some jokes are written outward from a particular pun, some lies are told backward from a particular euphemism, some promises are improvised forward from a particular misunderstanding.

Some words are more at home on the dry land of a dictionary than in the deep water of daily usage, or more comfortable preserved in etymological amber than randomly mutating on the contemporary tongue.

The parking space between Presently and Immediately has a meter that is impossible to feed coins into quickly enough. The elevator that goes from the ground floor of one's glossary to the mezzanine level of one's intended meaning runs on cables that are never quite connotative enough.

If humans were named for their vocalizations like certain birds are our field guides would contain references to Lost-Marble Warblers, Cross-Billed Curse-out Artists, Worry-Throated Whip-poor-wills, Loose-String Lyrebirds, and Stopped-Sinus Sandpipers.

A lie detector doesn't have a setting labeled "libel" because a lie producer doesn't have a sweat-gland labeled "slander." A cardiogram is a sentence that is all commas, colons, and assorted forms of continuance clicking until it is completed.

Sometimes a word engaged in a futile verbal enterprise is like a blowtorch taken to a blizzard. Sometimes a word is a still frame taken from the flipbook cinema of a sentence. Sometimes a sentence looks like it dressed itself in the dark and mismatched its grammatical attire.

How irregular can the past tense of a verb be before it is prehistoric? Halfway into forming a reluctant "hello," is a too-eager "farewell" already forming its foothold? Is a password ever so secret it can only be pronounced by a self-induced injury?

Every question's keyword implies a rhyming-word that is its existential host:
the all-surrounding air for "where"
and the sublime sky for "why"
a specific spot for "what" and a timely then for "when"
an all-inclusive you for "who" and a scapegoated id for "did."

☼◇☼◇ ☼◇☼◇ ☼◇☼◇☼◇☼◇☼◇☼◇☼

The stripes on a tiger's forehead form the character for the Chinese word wang or "king," but the worry-lines furrowed onto a human forehead can form any number of more ignoble words, depending on the cause of said furrows.

Japanese is read down a vertical column
like a pearl-diver plummeting for pictograms:
Arabic is read from right to left
like a sandstorm blowing in from the Further East:
Cuneiform was often read in a back-and-forth pattern
like a bull plowing the pasture of a page.

Write your signature in a pen that skips or hops and it is in danger of resembling a dotted line for someone else's signature. Keep adding names to your moniker and you'll only have a truly middle name with every other addition.

Sometimes the penultimate syllable of a word pumps its brakes before its punctuation kicks in. Sometimes the accents along the Dropped-R Riviera intersect with the accents along the Flattened-Vowel Panhandle.

§∞§∞§∞§∞§∞§∞§∞§∞§∞§∞§∞§∞§

The gap between the tidal hiss of a calligrapher's brush and the granular grind of a lead pencil is narrower than the gap between the rotary glide of a ballpoint pen and the clattering gamelan orchestra of a word-processing keyboard.

Try to encapsulate your entire outlook in a single word and that word will quickly take on so many prefixes, suffixes, and accent marks
that it will collapse like a syllabic soufflé.

Sometimes, the letter "y" seems to have half-passed and half-failed its audition to transfer from consonant housing to vowel housing. Sometimes, the letter "q" seems to revel in its relative autonomy in transliterated Arabic to compensate for its lean-to codependence on "u" in written English.

When an obsessively repeated word evaporates into nonsense on one's tongue, a few moments of suspended non-use are needed for said word to semantically "resume."

٥ʃ٥3٥ʃ٥3٥ʃ٥3٥ʃ٥3٥ʃ٥3٥ʃ٥3٥ʃ٥3٥ʃ٥3

Just as a cow can walk up a set of stairs but not down, some words can be assembled into a promise more easily than into a denial. Like a snake whose strike has the reach of half its body, the term "half-done" is half made up of "half."

When a Catholic's confirmation name is selected for its ability to undermine a resented first name or an outgrown surname, a baptismal name crumples its certificate and a marriage license winces in agreement.

Sometimes flamboyance in phrasing is foliage hiding an absence of fruit. Sometimes slang-ish semi-words hunker down and hide when the scouts for next year's dictionary come poking around.

The most defiant of plagiarists disables his quotation-mark key and the most decisive of liars disables his ellipses-maker and the bluntest of oath-takers disables his commas.

Every metaphor knows intuitively that the loops of cursive writing are lariats and lassoes hurled out to snare the ankles of fugitive figures of expression.

Sometimes a four-letter profanity under its own self-interrogation reveals itself to be one-quarter Rage and one quarter Defiance one-quarter Misstep and one-quarter Half-Meant.

In terms of an assonant existentialism the existence of eyelets allows us to be unlaced just as the existence of eye-drops allows us to be unlubricated.

When one's mental censor prematurely wears out its brake-pads on minor offenses, it weakens its anti-locking braking-distance for preventing a major faux pas when it approaches. When an insincere letter of recommendation winces at its own adjectives, a too-sincere love letter groans over its own adverbs.

Sometimes figurative language is a fig-leaf folded in front of Freud's forbidden-fruit basket. Sometimes a Jungian slip is telling an optometrist you need collective lenses instead of corrective lenses.

Perhaps a carcass "lingers" from the perspective of a buzzard and a cadaver "loiters" from the perspective of a forensic scientist where a corpse merely "lies" from the perspective of a mortician.

Sometimes a word wears a figurative press-card in its hatband to reinforce its credentials and a lint-sized micro-camera on its lapel to conceal its double-agency.

A wine-spill resembling someone's signature and a peacock-plume able to pass as someone's retinal scan and a haphazard keysmash that replicates someone's password are stumbled-onto signals wearing the accidental attire of Intention.

The barbed-wire barricade that a noun sets up between itself and certain adjectives is never fully impregnable. The deep-water moat that a verb digs between itself and certain adverbs waits to be crossed by the gangway plank of gutter-talk. The grammatical guardrails along a sentence's contour steer recommended word-usage into road-wise word-traffic.

A shrinking-closet paragraph used to slam closed a horror-story uses a too-perfect present tense to patrol its perimeter and an asteroid belt of an ellipsis to enclose its outer limits….

How fine can a fine print be before it is a footnote in powder form? How dotted can a dotted line be before it is its own ellipses? How creative can mishearing be before it is "impressionistic ignoring"?

Occasionally the words in a clause attain such camaraderie they palpably long to coalesce into an amalgamated superword. Occasionally a semicolon goes asleep at the switch and allows a sentence's syntax to slip past itself.

《±《±《±《±《±《±《±《±《±《±《±《±《±《±《±《±《±《±《±

When the "ou" that goes missing in "y'all" finds itself down the same vowel-drain as the dropped second "e" in "every," a certain kind of syllable slippage continues its spiral.

A buzzword humbly returned to its hive
becomes a honeyed endearment
a loanword overlooking its own interest-rate
learns to self-inflate,
a password patrolled by its own past tense
presents itself as protected
and a crossword puzzle undermined by its own clues
auto-corrects its answer-key.

When our globe has a West Pole and an East Pole, its newly vertical equator will slice a few now-regional dialects and once-national accents in two.

The shape of the word "shape" knows when to wind like a snake and when to drop a descender like a kickstand. The outline of the word "outline" knows why a compound word best suits its objectives. The contour of the word "contour" knows some of the supportive and subliminal effects of a repeated vowel.

Every direct object knows in its own way why the feet "take" steps but the hands "make" gestures and why the feet "make" tracks but the hands "take" hold.

Sometimes an "officer" becomes an "agent" where a "border" becomes a "barricade" and "offending" becomes "unbecoming" where an "inelegance" becomes an "annoyance."

Some participles merely dangle, while some sway back and forth like a gallows-hanged criminal. Some comma splices place a kink in a sentence's continuum, while some roll over a run-on and allow it to reciprocate.

In corporate network news, what appears to be "running commentary" is often merely "rolling-downhill commentary." In global espionage novels, a sentence that positions its subject and object in different time zones pays a punishing kind of postage on transitive verbs.

⸱≽⸱≽⸱≽⸱≽⸱≽⸱≽⸱≽⸱≽⸱≽⸱≽⸱≽⸱≽⸱≽⸱≽⸱≽⸱≽⸱≽

Sometimes the silence on the front end of a sentence cannot afford to be as deafening as the silence at the back end of that same sentence. Sometimes co-dependent clauses cry out for the couples-counseling only a semicolon can provide.

When the language barrier between a native tongue and its newcomers is made steeper by its idioms and wider by its ironies, said barrier is also made narrower by its expletives and shallower by its hand-signs.

In terms of inner images, our verbal brain can easily picture "unraveling" and "undressing" but has a harder time picturing "unpicturing" or "unpurposing" and an impossible time picturing what an act of 'impossibling' would look like.

Sometimes a greeting card is actually an avoidance card because sometimes a calling card is recalled in favor of a formerly-known-as card.

Learn to speak a second language past the age of forty and your nouns will be more reliable than your verbs, your articles will be more decisive than your adjectives, and your subjunctives will be moodier than your imperatives. Enter a boiler-basement full of telemarketers and you'll hear many more adjectives than qualifiers and many more absolutes than conditionals per hour.

The word "actually" is an enemy of analogies because it encourages idioms to be as self-evident as images and utterances to be as undeniable as effigies.

When a fictional character is as close to its writer as that writer is to her editor and that editor is to his publisher, a printer should dwell as close to a paper-mill as that paper-mill does to a logging-camp.

When an asterisk is a miniature supernova-in-the-making a footnote is a fact's root cellar in a state of fungal riot and a displaced diacritical mark is a fugitive looking for a willing vowel to roost on.

☼◇☼◇☼◇☼◇☼◇☼◇☼◇☼◇☼

The grammatical equivalent of a U-turn is necessitated by a preposition pile-up as frequently as by a connotation collision. In a game of dominoes played with word-bearing instead of dot-bearing tiles, "effect" can topple "cause" just as much as vice versa.

When selecting translucent gemstones to use as scriptural reading-lenses, use a belligerent bloodstone to read *The Art of War* and a full dilated tiger's-eye to read the visionary summits of the *Rig-Veda* and an undistorting diamond to read the bracing maxims of the *Tao Te Ching*.

The coins in a velvet-lined guitar case can be easily arranged to spell the word "donate," but the change in a passerby's pocket can't easily form into the word "non-spare."

Some syllables are surface-to-air missiles percussed on a tongue and deflected off a palate. Some syllables are subtitles used as time-saving devices. Some syllables hint of journalese trying too hard to join its fellow jargons.

§∞§∞§∞§∞§∞§∞§∞§∞§∞§∞§∞§

The word "verbose" causes one to lean away from one's dictionary as surely as the word "overdrawn" causes one to lean away from one's debit-card. The word "erosive" is less erosive to a pencil's lead than the word "accumulative," but harder to erase than the word "blank."

Sometimes a not-so-innocent questionnaire comes with an implied naked light bulb hanging above it. Sometimes the drawing-board for a certain would-be word collapses under the burden of its undertaking. Sometimes a horse's hoof can spell out a small vocabulary of words but hollers on "stampede" and stammers on "gelatine."

In terms of unintentional orthography, a flattened mosquito that turns a two of spades into a three of spades is every bit as accidental a character as the letter "x" formed in the air while trying to swat that same mosquito.

The triangle formed by a three-word song-title tends to be more obtuse than the triangle formed by a three-word traffic sign but more acute than the triangle formed by a three-word food-label.

◁ʃ▷ ▷ʃ◁ ◁ʃ▷ ▷ʃ◁ ◁ʃ▷ ▷ʃ◁ ◁ʃ▷ ▷ʃ◁

The whistle of a boiling kettle of water moves diagonally across the vowels from a simmering "a" to a vaguely agitated "o" to an ascendant "i" to a shrieking "e." The two-humped "m" in "camel" and the spot-like "o" in "leopard" are in negotiations with the ear-evoking double "b" in "rabbit."

> Sighing is one of our sub-verbal spells
> against being transfixed by the Sublime:
> Sneering is one of our semi-vocal hexes
> against being too dependent on Sentiment:
> Wincing is one of our facial mantras
> against being mangled by Worry.

Is being "deprereflected" a matter of having one's prior status in a mirror nullified? Is being "antiunexasperated" a matter of opposing an absence of impatience? Is "quasiantivaccinated" a pretense at being opposed to being prepared for an epidemic?

"Till tomorrow…" is a promise but "To be continued…" a warning only during times of "Someday soon…" being a reassurance but "Any moment now…" being an omen.

For reasons verbal and visual, a society in which prosecutors were as likely to write haiku as defense attorneys were likely to write novels would be as forgiving as one in which prosecutors were as likely to paint watercolors as defense attorneys were likely to sculpt monuments.

The term-limits of a term of endearment prevent it from re-running for ardor-proclaiming office. A promise sworn on a motel bible is as mobile and versatile as a trucker's trailer-hitch. A vow attested to in gestures is as posture-dependent as it is post-verbal.

The Bible one brings to bed and the bestseller one brings to the beach are allowed to disagree on how ultimately binding a book's spine needs to be.

The difference between "relentless" and "unrelenting" is in degrees-of-pursuit but "uncaring" is more proactive than "careless" and "carefree" combined and "unending" is to "open-ended" as "endless" is to "eternal."

⸻

Any book can be turned into a pleated and folded accordion format, but not just any book can be played at the Trevi fountain as accompaniment to the cavorting antics of a squirrel monkey in a pillbox hat and a tasseled vest.

A portmanteau formed from ancient Hebrew and Welsh would have no storage compartment for vowels. A Romance-derived *r*-sound can be so rolled it serves as bait for rattlesnakes. A trans-Siberian pun can be so extensive its syllables cover four different time zones.

An opening sentence that blends salutation and sign-off leaves a letter with little else to do. A robotic arm programmed to write an unmeant suicide note is committing an act of pseudo-sorrow, demi-despair, and non-nullity.

If kissing the Blarney Stone is an Irish eloquence-enhancer, kissing Plymouth Rock is an American irony-inhibitor. Regardless of stone-kissing, many people's italicized sarcasm-voice has a wider and deeper vocabulary than their in-brackets confidentiality-voice or their bold-font sincerity-voice.

The air-traffic controller for a wedding vow
    waves in certain adjectives
  and waves away certain adverbs
  and warns a particular qualifier
it will need to orbit the tarmac indefinitely.

"Please" used as a single-word pseudo-sentence is frequently a longer request in its dried pellet form, while "Don't" used as a pseudo-sentence is frequently a longer prohibition in its just-add-water state.

Can a word be an ingredient in Old English's anti-aging cream and part of the antidote to Middle English's mid-life crisis and an ice-crystal in Modern English's cryogenic suspension all at once?

Our "wordiness" is more specifically "nouniness" when we are waxing materialistic and "verbiness" when we are waxing hyperactive. When hitting verbosity's outer limits, one can hit rewind on a half-meant remark and end up mummified in unspooled tape.

《±《±《±《±《±《±《±《±《±《±《±《±《±《±《±

The word "set" requires so much space to be fully defined by a dictionary it drives an even wider wedge between the words "saved" and "sinful."

Editors learn to:
hike a sentence up a flagpole and check it for flutter:
drop it down a crater and check it for plummet
or sew it into a sweater and check it for monogram.

How segmented a drone needs to be before it is a discussion isn't determined by how sustained a staccato can be before it is a dirge. The gestures our shadows least want to reflect and the words our echoes least want to repeat might not be as related as we might imagine.

For reasons both syntactical and self-serving, the person who is most articulate when describing the precise place his back needs scratching is often least eloquent when describing why his fingers grow tired so quickly when massaging someone else.

The subject-object-verb order of an action-postponing Japanese sentence can depict a tea-kettle made to bubble as resonantly as a mountain-river and a coffeemaker evoking a rush-hour scramble for a subway car.

The more deadly bureaucratic the noun, the more likely the Pentagon will activate it as a verb with a "-ing" or an "-ed." The more grimly lethal the verb, the more likely the Pentagon will smother it into a noun with a "-ment" or "-ity" or "-tion" or "-ure."

Telling off its own surrounding words is a weapons-grade profanity's version of target practice. Flattering its fellow phrase-members is a euphemism's way of arranging a statement into objective agreement.

An accent can't be trademarked by an enclave because a piece of slang can't be patented by a street-corner and a cliché can't be copyrighted by a clique.

≳ἰ≳ἰ≳ἰ≳ἰ≳ἰ≳ἰ≳ἰ≳ἰ≳ἰ≳ἰ≳ἰ≳ἰ≳ἰ≳ἰ≳ἰ

If Native Alaskans truly did have hundreds of words for different kinds of snow, they might also have a sibilant-stuffed word for "slippery," a quick-to-flee interjection for "polar bear," a glare-proof adjective for "midnight sun," and only an interrupted half-word for "avalanche."

Sometimes a name can be dropped with such poor timing that it plummets endlessly down a bottomless abyss. Sometimes a hint can be dropped with such a lack of nuance that its splashdown occurs before it is fully spoken.

Sometimes our speech-instrument is so out of tune it emits the word "correction" when our mental bow-stroke clearly called for "error" and dispenses the word "harmony" when our mental strum clearly called for "discord."

In a 3D hologrammar each sentence will no longer be a line but a Platonic solid each period will be a sphere and each dash a bar a comma spun on its axis will cut in half what is used to connect-as-one each sentence's diagram tree will cast off leaves no rake can retrieve.

Our studies of syntax are too often paleontologies rather than vivisections—studies of the fossilized skeleton instead of the soft and generating tissues. We should never trust the success of a science (or a sentence) that doesn't contain the seeds of its own subversion.

When "second-in-line" sneaks up on "standing alone," a sentence's sense of sequence has been jump-started. When our body English has an accent so battered it is the overused brake-pedal on our anatomy's eloquence, eye-contact goes looking for its own idiomatic elbow-room.

Our most common verb ("be") is also our most irregular in its tenses, as if its overexposed omnipresence caused it to seek out the disguises of "were" and "am" and "is."

Contemplate the names of Fibonacci or Euclid or Descartes at a Las Vegas casino and ten anti-card-counting security scanners will peer ever-deeper into your brain-stem transmissions. Contemplate the names of Darwin or Mendel or Lamarck at a hotel bar and your genetic intentions will be probed.

In the non-verbal language of injured objects, sometimes the air howling out of a puncture is an agoraphobic protest, sometimes it is a moan of claustrophobic relief. In our own non-verbal orality, we evolve from merely "feeding" to "eating" to eventually "dining" as our "grub" turns into "food" turns into "cuisine."

Speaking fluent civil unrest sometimes means throwing an Esperanto cocktail into a bookstore. Speaking fluent grammar-goaltending means being a gate-keeper and a guardian at once. Speaking fluent punctuation means knowing a semicolon segregates what a comma quarantines.

If the roulette wheel of writing has better odds of landing on a pictogram than on a hieroglyph when spun from east to west, it has better odds of landing on a letter than on an icon when spun from west to east.

The "u" in "unroofed" is a roofless version of its two "o"'s-to-come. The "e"'s in "eye" are a pair of half-lidded pupils serving a palindrome. The "i" in "infrared" is as eye-eluding as the "i" in "iridescent" is eye-enhancing.

§∞§∞§∞§∞§∞§∞§∞§∞§∞§∞§∞§∞§

Which letter would benefit most from being turned into a 3D hologram: the O that would convert into a sphere or the lower-case l that would turn into a pillar or the capital E that would turn into a cage?

The ultimate hallucination of the aphorist: a book pirouetting so fast on its spine that it has more words than letters and more sentences than words and more paragraphs than sentences and more chapters than paragraphs.

We can "tell time" but not ultimately tell time from space because can we "pay lip service" but not pay lip service a steady salary and can "give grief" but not give grief its own job title.

The U.S. Constitution's 25 pages have had to bear more burden-of-proof-per-page than any document since the Book of Genesis. The American Declaration of Independence's parchment has already endured more skeptical cross-examination than the Dead Sea Scrolls have endured carbon-dating analysis. The First Amendment is a font of friction as well as freedom because the Second Amendment is a source of swagger as well as security.

⌂ʃ⌂ ⌂ʃ⌂ ⌂ʃ⌂ ⌂ʃ⌂ ⌂ʃ⌂ ⌂ʃ⌂ ⌂ʃ⌂ ⌂ʃ⌂

At the intersection of Lowered Eyes and Upraised Eyebrows, collisions between head-on coquettishness and half-meant surprise are not unusual.

A book underlining its own references to ferocity in yellow and its own remarks on cowardice in red has a color-coding index based on Conundrum.

There are certain passive nouns that obediently sigh when placed next to an adjective like "maudlin" but defiantly groan when placed next to an adjective like "grandiose." There are adverbs that perform deep, syllabic knee-bends when placed next to a verb like "unfurl" and perform the hatha yoga corpse asana when placed next to a verb like "unwind."

    Some Caribbean dialects turn a statement into a question by ending in a terminal "hey," while some American dialects turn a confession into an accusation by letting "hey" be its own sentence.

The heliotrope version of a verb goes from "will [blank]" to "[blank]ing" to "has [blank]ed"
    as the sun of its syntax moves across the sky.

    A calendar with a daily image for each synonym for "synonym" would become ironic long before it became annual. A quadrilingual advice-column would quickly learn that some misbehaviors are easier to defend in French than in Spanish, just as some self-contradictions are easier to avoid in German than in English.

If a love-letter took as long to dry as a Jackson Pollock canvas, our global population would be considerably smaller. If a suicide note took as long to chisel as a Henry Moore sculpture, our global populations would be slightly larger.

  In the politics of the prefix
 regruntling the disgruntled is a heroic act
while rebunking the debunked is an act of cowardice.

Statistically, the word most likely to be emitted immediately following a "swig" from a coffee mug tends to be more critical and impatient than the word most likely to be uttered following a "sip" from a teacup.

A language invented by a civil engineer
 would have aqueducts for its vowels
  and brace-fittings for its consonants
   and suspension bridges for its conjunctions.

An alternative version of Rodin's *The Thinker* holding a pen would compromise its fist's ability to prop its own mouth closed. An alternative version of the *Venus de Milo* holding a pen would require a back-handed disamputation.

The phrase "also known as" has palindromic initials to allow two-way traffic between one's actual name and one's alias. The spelling of the word "oscillator" contains a pair of wormholes and a pair of parallel columns that allow the word's appearance to underscore its meaning.

Try to read a secular text through a stained-glass monocle and its reasonableness will be tinted into a post-Rapture rainbow. Try to hold a profanity under your tongue for too long and it will eventually curdle your saliva but enhance your peptic acid.

The word "four" names the number of letters in its name as accurately as the word "one" names its number of syllables, but the numeral "1" can be mistaken for the lower-case "l" in "lone" more easily than "4" can be mistaken for "quartet"'s lower-case "q."

The "Is this on?" spoken into a microphone tends to be more confident and less tentative than the one spoken into a voice recorder because an utterance is often energized by its addressees.

If the crescent moon on a sorcerer's hat were actually a capital C, said monogram would have Conjurer, Cultist, and Clairvoyant among its candidates.

《±

When a word grows too accustomed to doing its work half-awake it needs the steep precipice of prolonged silence to surprise itself out of its semantic slumber.

Sometimes a sentence's steering wheel converts to a turn ratio of two verbs per noun when it hits especially rutted mental terrain. Sometimes a comma is a rubber door-stop preventing the door-slam of a more terminal punctuation.

When we crumple a piece of paper as a gesture of dismissal, we spatially promote said paper from a two-dimensional to a three-dimensional state.

If we write "Don't believe my flipside" both upside down and right-side-up on both surfaces of a piece of paper, we perform a semantic pirouette and barrel-roll at once.

Some sentences are houndstooth in their grammar and some are herringbone, depending on how they interlace their nouns and verbs and how their phrasing's fabric invites certain word-weaves.

Dogmatism is bred by placing the word "belief" in our blind-spot and the word "doubt" in our deaf-spot and the word "mixture" in our mute-spot.

Sometimes a last name gains a syllable during a civil war's peace negotiations and loses that same syllable during the immigration process. Sometimes when a whispered aside escapes from the prison of its muffling parentheses it reaches for the nearest exclamation point.

If war epics are written from the shoulder
novellas are written from the elbow
sonnets from the wrist
and haiku from the fingertips.

In a mass bibliocide in which every book determines its own mode of self-murder, detective novels would be strangled with a call-girl's satin garter and Gothic romances would be tossed off a moss-overgrown parapet into a foaming and tumescent cataract.

Some action-verbs (like "elocute" and "articulate")
are adverb-incubators
while some (like "erase" and "annihilate")
are adverb-extinguishers
and some (like "waver" and "vacillate")
are adverb-adjusters.

How long can "unquote" delay its arrival before an ellipsis needs to enter and adjudicate? How much muter is the "woof" of a cable-woven sweater than the "bark" of a giant redwood? Does placing a criminal confession inside an echo chamber risk blurring the line between "felonious" and "fabricated"?

The words "Wash Me" can easily be written on a dusty surface but the words "Stop Washing Me" can find no finger-hold on a too-clean surface.

↓ḋ↓ḋ↓ḋ↓ḋ↓ḋ↓ḋ↓ḋ↓ḋ↓ḋ↓ḋ↓ḋ↓ḋ↓ḋ↓

The second "b" in "bomb"'s muteness, in contrast to its initial, enunciated "b," seems to underscore the word "bomb"'s silencing-power.

Water flowing over stone is a reassurance and a stone dropped into water is an interrogative. Water pooling and shimmering atop a stone is an adjective and a stone being eroded by water is a derogatory. Water steaming from a stone is an evasion and a stone cracking under frozen water is in the passive voice.

An omnivore Adam entrusted to name the plants instead of the animals would enunciate those names more on his molars than on his incisors.

Homme and "homicidal" were on very intimate terms long before *femme* was introduced to *fatale,* but "assassin"'s quartet of "s"'s joined together as a conspiracy independent of "murder"'s own self-rhyming.

☼◇☼◇☼◇☼◇☼◇☼◇☼◇☼◇☼

Over-pronouncing the term "ill-defined" with too much hard palate doesn't undercut its own meaning in quite the same the way that under-pronouncing the term "precision-tooled" with too little tooth, tongue, and tonsil would.

How many of the million names of God are prefabricated titles assembled by vested monopolies, how many are cosmically misspelled crossword responses, how many are initials in search of an anagram, and how many are desperate and ill-aimed stabs into the Silence?

When a diary starts resembling a dictionary, one's daily impressions are too intense in their need for definition. When a romance novel starts resembling a repair manual, a market share has grown muddled by its readership's motivation.

"Adjective" may mean "tossed toward"
but many modifiers creep toward a noun on padded feet
or arc slow and gentle across a semantic sky
before landing on an intended target.

§∞§∞§∞§∞§∞§∞§∞§∞§∞§∞§∞§∞§∞§∞§

If a codebreaker stares at a grammar-guide long enough, he will come to realize that if a verb is an echo cast by an action, a noun is a shadow cast by an object, and an adjective is a ripple cast by a quality.

If a witness sworn in on a newspaper were half as reliable as a witness sworn in on a Bible, he would presumably still be twice as reliable as a witness sworn in on a car-wash coupon.

A comma closely resembles a sperm-cell both visually and in its function as a continuer of a line. The word AND, as an anagrammatic rearrangement of DNA, is involved in a related irony.

A ten-page-long palindrome tends to lose sight of its center pivot long before it loses sight of its two opposing poles and tends to favor bilaterally symmetrical letters like o and x and w over letters whose lopsidedness intrude on its spell of self-reflection.

⌂ʃ⌂ ⌂ʃ⌂ ⌂ʃ⌂ ⌂ʃ⌂ ⌂ʃ⌂ ⌂ʃ⌂ ⌂ʃ⌂ ⌂ʃ⌂

Sometimes a laboratory mouse halfway down an anaconda's gullet can resemble a too-bulky curse word halfway up a slanderer's vocal cords. Sometimes a slang-word is contraband smuggled across a dictionary's dividing line by a too-empowered trend.

There are some books that offer a reader more lyric legroom but less overhead mental-storage space than others. There are likewise books that offer a reclining seat for moments of idyllic reverie but also have their seatback tray-table permanently folded away in an upright position.

Some sentences leap off their assembly-line half-completed trailing nuts and bolts of foregone nuance and rivets of potential rewording while some sentences spend so much time on the factory floor their hinges rust shut and their syllables cry out for an oilcan.

If our spoken language could better depict the flickering and fleeting nuances of our inner minds, we would have evolved out of the need for archable and opposable eyebrows by now.

The word "endurance" would more accurately reflect its refusal to end if it were renamed "andurance." The word "continuum" would more accurately reflect its own carrying-on if its two successive *u*'s didn't contradict each other's pronunciations.

A skywriting plane practicing punctuation with its exhaust fumes has an easy, linear time with an ellipsis but needs to power-sweep to perform parentheses and barrel-roll to produce a bracket and cartwheel to emit a comma-splice.

Taking a large and emphatic bite out of a meal after you've been verbally interrupted is a matter of "conspicuous resumption." Pausing for an exaggerated interval in between jokes or bites are interrelated matters of jesting and ingesting.

> The denser a word's syllables-to-letters ratio is
> the more likely it will bruise its meaning's shins
> on its pronunciation's furniture
> and the less likely its alpine echo
> will return with every element intact.

For reasons both topical and tropical, Filipinos use the verb-phrase "sour graping" to refer to someone in a state of envy, but not "appling" for a temptress luring someone into original sin or "oranging" for an object whose pigment determines its name.

> The evergreen advice of "write drunk, edit sober"
> can also be phrased "write crackling, edit cooled"
> or "write ravaged, edit reassembled"
> or "write pulverized, edit pillowed."

What sort of semantic scalpel can separate an utterance's denotative yolk from its connotative albumen or its descriptive kernels from its prescriptive cob? What kind of a baby-rattle filled with commas, ellipses and semicolons instead of plastic beads would make for a more indecisive adulthood?

Self-Stalemating vs. Self-Scapegoating is the unwinnable argument a one-sided debate has to endure when a single speaker's burden of proof is balanced by her own burden of rejoinder and her ability to cross-examine her own rebuttals folds into a kind of intellectual origami.

A promise written in illegibly dull pencil can lead to an argument set down in indelibly unerasable ink. A negotiation started in lower-case lettering can climax in a disagreement boxed in by its own bold font.

The number of sentences in a barroom toast raised to a barely-known comrade should not exceed the number of ingredients in a scotch of average complexity. The number of words in a barely-veiled barroom threat should not exceed the number of shards the average shot glass breaks into.

Sometimes a synonym is more of an impersonator than an alternative, sometimes more of a supplement than a surrogate, and sometimes more of a devotee than a doppelganger.

The post-lovemaking pillow-poem that used to be expected of Japanese men couldn't mention being distracted by a pending business deal during the processes leading to climax nor hint at the ways that seduction itself is a matter of transaction and trade-dealing.

《土

For purposes of mood-control and in the name of an antonym's opposition research, "miserable" doesn't get a "miserific" as a counter-balance like "terrible" gets "terrific" (as an opponent) and "horrible" gets "horrific" (as an intensifier).

Sometimes an adjective is a half-unpeeled decal pasted slantways on a fast-moving noun's rear fender. Sometimes a paragraph is the verbal equivalent of a five-car garage pretending not to know whose fault an oil-stain is.

The *or*'s in "st*or*y," "l*or*e,' and "aph*or*ism" are unrelated despite their service as genre-labels, just as the *and*'s in "aggr*and*izement," "c*and*idacy," and "gerrym*and*er" are unrelated despite their service as political movers.

An ellipsis is a perforated stammering of not-quite full-stops a drumroll triplet of pivots in uniform sequence and a model of just how fine a fine print can get before it turns into a dotted line…

⸙⸙⸙⸙⸙⸙⸙⸙⸙⸙⸙⸙⸙⸙⸙⸙⸙⸙⸙⸙⸙⸙⸙⸙⸙

If the lower-case l and the numeral 1 are alphanumeric allies, the upper-case L and the numeral 7 are alphanumeric antipodes. If a direct object's suction tries to meet a transitive verb's outflow, it occasionally requires an adjective adjustment to dilate its nozzle.

Frequently, a sigh is the busy signal we get when we mis-dial the word "silence." Occasionally, the letters on a keyboard that fade from overuse spell out an invisible mantra.

A haiku placed on a slide projector is always seventeen clicks away from returning to its season of origin, just as a sonnet jammed into a Ten Commandments template is always four prohibitions past overspill.

Restless Adverb Syndrome is a modifier ailment that suffers a telltale quiver in the deep fibers of its "questioningly," a nerve-knotting twitch in the synapses of its "tremblingly," and a tell-all spasm in the unmassaged regions of its "seemingly."

≻i≻i≻i≻i≻i≻i≻i≻i≻i≻i≻i≻i≻i≻i≻i≻i

When a Greek chorus becomes a Roman chorus, its running commentary is more military and less metaphysical. When doublespeak allows itself to be divided in two, it becomes half-committed instead of bipartisan.

Since the words "shears" and "tongs" are rarely used in the singular, a single tool that was half-shear and half-tong at once would be both anatomically and semantically lopsided.

When "free" speech realizes it can be furloughed from the prison of platitude, it forgets it can just as easily be imprisoned in the gulag of mere gossip. When an acronym can no longer be pronounced as a freestanding word, it sacrifices its status and returns to the rank-and-file of abbreviations.

Unpeeling is easier than unslivering
because dismounting is easier than disfalling:
Misapplying is easier than mis-healing
because every antibody
opposes absolute auto-immunity:
Quasi-counterfeited is a coiled helix
because pseudo-simulated is a spiraled corkscrew.

↓d↓d↓d↓d↓d↓d↓d↓d↓d↓d↓d↓d↓d↓d↓d↓

Sometimes a resignation letter gets more frenetic with each successive paragraph until its commas are leapfrogging its dashes and its exclamation points are lying face down in a pool of scratched-out profanities.

If truly seeing an object temporarily dislocates it from its name,
half-forgetting an object's name will make for a more vivid item,
and mispronouncing certain words brings new objects into Being.

When confirmation bias can find probable cause inside of a trigger warning, too many two-word idioms have imposed their competing polarities upon a single sentence.

When the eager and hopeful apostrophe one-third of the way through the word "I'll" comes upon the weary and evasive apostrophe three-quarters of the way through the word "can't," a conflict between intent and ability ensues.

☼◇☼◇☼◇☼◇☼◇☼◇☼◇☼◇☼

The half-unmeant part of a half-meant insult can't claim credit for the verbs and claim innocence for the nouns. Our "profanity footprint" likewise can't ask to be gauged in terms of its carbon dioxide-to-curse-word ratio.

Pluralize the word "infinity" and uniqueness itself grows anxious.
Singularize the word "loggerheads" and an argument loses its objective.
Itemize the word "collective" and outliers start looking for exit strategies.

Sometimes an adjective is the fly-spatter on a noun trying to be as transparent as a windshield and sometimes it is a cross made of masking tape to prevent a nearly transparent noun from being walked into.

The "hem-lock" that killed Socrates suggests a device for clamping down on the fringe of an unraveling garment, which is what the killing of Socrates was—a civic flyswatting that didn't foresee that gadfly extermination is a never-ending, self-renewing process.

§∞§∞§∞§∞§∞§∞§∞§∞§∞§∞§∞§∞§

When -isms spasm, entire states of being wriggle in ontological distress. When a self-correcting text stubs its toe on a slang-term or pulls a tendon on an idiom, the entire notion of verbal hygiene is combat-tested.

If a "spanagram" is a mile-wide set of initials, a "slangover" is the weariness a tongue feels from having used too many trending terms and a "blundertow" is the gravitational force exerted by one's accumulated verbal errors.

A trade name that has passed into general usage no longer needs the billy-club of an exclamation mark to make its point. The words "salon" and "boutique" and "bistro" are all self-flattering moniker upgrades that venues unilaterally grant themselves.

      While air-quotes can induce irony
an air-cross-out only partially cancels a regretted word,
      and an air-ellipsis is only sometimes
              an utterance's anti-lock braking system.

⌂ʃ⌂ ⌂ʃ⌂ ⌂ʃ⌂ ⌂ʃ⌂ ⌂ʃ⌂ ⌂ʃ⌂ ⌂ʃ⌂ ⌂ʃ⌂

      The invention of the plate-glass window led to the invention of the advertising slogan. The discovery of the subatomic particle gave new life to gerunds like "timing" and "spacing." The invention of the alphabet gave the swarming mass of Meaning its single-file marching orders.

    If "jawboning" refers to idle talk
        and "double-tonguing" to a saxophone technique,
      "upper lipping" is an exercise in decorum
and "mandibling" refers to an underbite on overdrive.

An ideal "ear conditioning" unit would feature a Mozart Massage Mode as well as a Shakespeare Endearment Gear, an Idiomatic Overdrive and a Tower of Babel Tuning-Fork, a Decibel Dampening-Pedal and a White-Noise Wordlessness feature.

Irregular plurals like "agendum" and "alumnae" and "codices" compete in a blue-ribbon contest for most exotic tail-end, while prefixes like "mal-" and "dys-," "contra-" and "anti-," "omni-" and "pan-," and "multi-" and "poly-" continue their Greco-Roman wrestling.

Periods have different degrees of what pistol-vendors call "stopping power," depending on their punctuational "caliber." Likewise, exclamation marks come with different degrees of emphasis depending on their posture and question marks with different degrees of striking-distance depending on their ability to uncoil.

The British not placing periods after the abbreviations Dr, Mr, and Mrs doesn't necessarily lead to a more open-ended sense of Self just as tactically inserting a Lord before or an Esquire after doesn't necessarily bestow a preface or postmark upon a name.

Some surveillance dossiers get so declassified they become the basis for international ad campaigns and Times Square billboards. Some forms of artificial intelligence come pre-blended with their own artificial ignorance, artificial disinterest and artificial obsession to balance themselves out.

The adverb "hereby" applied to "decree" or "announce" is ceremonially pompous but a "forthwith" applied to "hint" or "suggest" is logically incompatible and a "thusly" applied to "curse" or "damn" is suffering from delusions of sorcery.

──────────────────────────────

There are words that prove that "please" is not the only mule capable of pulling the cart called Petition and words that deny that "promise" is the only hand-grip capable of closing the door called Pledge.

The midwestern accent of a tornado flattens its own freestanding vowels. A hurricane's tropical intonation rolls its consonants in warm-front crosswinds. A monsoon's liquid consonants flood its low-lying territories in a tidal tongue-tying.

A stickler who replaces the word "snow" with the word "sand" in every Christmas carol ever written renders the holiday songbook more historically accurate and less commercially feasible at once.

A Conspiracy of One is a "cahoot" in the singular
    only if a singular "kudo" is a half-intended applause
        and an unaccompanied "paparazzo" is a Cyclops
           and a sole piece of "confetto"
    is a paper-particle separated from its swarm.

Our language may speak us and our books read us, but our wardrobe only wears us once our nakedness disowns us. Our vocabulary, like our other harvesting tools, makes itself most conspicuous when it breaks or bends during an assigned task.

A pearl made out of perjury forms under the tongue of a police informant at the same rate that a sequin made out of slander grows in the gullet of a gossip columnist.

A "quilt" is named for how it is joined together just as a "milkshake" is named for how it is combined, but a "woodchip" is named for how it is fragmented from its collective and a "snowflake" is named for its flamboyant state of independence. "Firewood" is named for the thing that consumes it and "hardwood" for the quality it possesses and "Hollywood" for the plant it displaced.

The phrase "my wife of many years" can be an endearment but "my wife of many decades" sounds like a complaint and "my wife of many hours" like a clear case of anxiety.

《±《±《±《±《±《±《±《±《±《±《±《±《±《±

The upper-case A, with its upward steeple,
    resents having to stand for the lower-depths "Abyss"
    as surely as the letter C, as an incomplete orb,
resents having to stand for the fully-rounded "Circuit."

The word "incognito" puts on earplugs every time its pronunciation gets mangled. The word "grunt" gnaws out of its gag-order every time grammar accuses it of glibness.

In the blurring of modern nomenclatures, the difference between a comments section and a customer reviews column is about as indistinct as the difference between a how-to manual and a user's guide.

Since the word "deferential" bows from its neck and "punctilious" bows from its waist "humble" must logically bow all the way to its knees and "obsequious" needs to somehow bow to the point of self-burial.

⸪⸪⸪⸪⸪⸪⸪⸪⸪⸪⸪⸪⸪⸪⸪⸪⸪⸪⸪⸪⸪⸪

The ampersand's early expulsion from our alphabet left several candidates campaigning for the position of 27th letter, including a hieroglyph for a whistle, an icon for molar-click, and a character for a lip-smack.

In between the "vida" and the "loca" falls the knuckle-rapping yardstick of orthodoxy. In between the "ad" and the "hominem" falls the shadow of slander. In between the "déjà" and the "vu" falls the eclipse of anticipation.

If "Kafkaesque" applied to a clinical trial and "Orwellian" applied to an odd-numbered calendar year ever agreed to switch places, "Dickensian" applied to a Detroit assembly line and "Machiavellian" applied to a manipulated-data climate conference wouldn't necessarily agree to remain in place.

The two "t"'s in "ditto"
  and two "d"'s in "addition"
    and two "x"'s in "Xerox"
      are comrades-in-appropriateness
       and sextuplets-in-irony.

꙳i꙳i꙳i꙳i꙳i꙳i꙳i꙳i꙳i꙳i꙳i꙳i꙳i꙳i꙳i

   The tongue is the hardest muscle to relax and the inner ear's bones are the hardest to surgically alter, two facts that must inflect our conversations greatly.

When free-falling in zero-gravity conversational space
  grabbing hold of a noun isn't always preferable
   to rappelling off a verb
    and barrel-rolling with an ellipsis
isn't always easier than skidding with serial commas.

Double its vowels and our language will ululate like a skylark gargling liquid air. Double its consonants and it will clatter like a drought-dried grasshopper's untrimmed cuticles.

Halve our bilabials and our speech will smack less of self-satisfaction. Halve our gutturals and our speech's groundwork will lose much of its formative gravel.

↓ȧ↓ȧ↓ȧ↓ȧ↓ȧ↓ȧ↓ȧ↓ȧ↓ȧ↓ȧ↓ȧ↓ȧ↓ȧ↓ȧ↓ȧ↓ȧ↓

Words of more than three syllables are most likely to break the spell that a lullaby weaves, and so the word "lullaby" itself requires three liquid "l"'s to soften its own impact.

Since reading a repair manual is more likely to cause one's lips to move than reading a romance novel is, what does a detective novel need to do to raise more eyebrows than a diary does?

Corrective lenses so corrective they convert a comma-splice into a continuum can also slow a run-on sentence to a steadier pace and detect when a letter's line of duty has formed an angle oblique to its own enunciation.

Profanity's limousine has its trunk popped open
    by a speed-bump set up by a censor
        a pothole dug by four-star four-letter word
and a hairpin turn in a slang-dictionary's foldout map.

☼◇☼◇☼◇☼◇☼◇☼◇☼◇☼◇☼

When a sentence tries too hard to become an enduring monument, it becomes a graffiti-magnet for syntax-vandals and a nest for grammatical pigeons. When a sentence is a concentrated nugget of a manifesto, guerrillas learn to add water and stir.

The censored sentences that a cork-lined room absorbs and the forbidden sentences that a lead-lined chamber deflects sometimes intersect in the rhetorical angles of a geodesic dome erected over a crater caused by a deep-impact profanity.

We all have different verbal recipes for guiding a driver into a parking space: some heavy on the iambs and encouragement, some heavy on the trochees and warnings, and some with wordless cries accompanied by a gestural rhetoric that only a rear-view mirror can recognize.

The "of course" that isn't alarmed by its own obviousness and the "of course not…" that can't awaken from its own oblivion intersect at an angle only apparent to each other's antidote.

§∞§∞§∞§∞§∞§∞§∞§∞§∞§∞§∞§

The "Qwerty" formed by a typewriter's upper row seems like a hybrid between an obscure adjective, a semi-anagram brand moniker and a diminutive nickname for an elderly aunt.

Some adjectives-of-reassurance clip our semantic alarm-wires. Some adverbs pull the flying carpet out from under a self-levitating verb. Some terms of endearment avoid being trademarked by flouting any sense of formula.

Because "pitch" and "volume" are distant relatives at best, one can raise and deepen one's voice at once by increasing its loudness and lowering its tone. Because "profanity" and "obscenity" are non-identical siblings, certain curse-words walking the line between the frowned-on and the forbidden.

The French refer to the "at" sign (@) as an escargot, and poet Richard Wilbur noticed that the ampersand looks like a miniature lyre. The exclamation point awaits someone to recognize its relation to a billy-club as surely as the question mark conceals its kinship with a plume of smoke.

◊∫◊ ◊∫◊ ◊∫◊ ◊∫◊ ◊∫◊ ◊∫◊ ◊∫◊ ◊∫◊

In the quantum field of auxiliary verbs, the molecular bonds between "may" and "might" are based on a different verbal valence and rhetorical repulsion than the atomic orbitals interlinking "can" and "could."

For reasons of syllabic time-management and ease-of-transition, our collective speech's daily ration of "and" seems to exceed our yearly portion of "furthermore" by roughly the same proportion that our hourly ration of "but" seems to dwarf our monthly portion of "nevertheless."

The tittle above a lower-case "j" and the tittle above a lower-case "i" are two miniature footprints in a word like "jitterbug" and a pair of sleigh-bells in a word like "jingle" and two items in absolute agreement in a word like "jibe."

If the word "ascetic" is the wool pulled over our ids, then "effacement" is the glossy-weave satin pulled over our egos, and "indolence" is the Blue Nile cotton pulled over our aspirations.

An attention span on the installment plan is needed to read an encyclopedia as if it were an epic poem. An attention span as patient as a UN teleprompter knows that what loiters and lingers in translation is trying to avoid getting lost.

If certain books have overheard the Bible better than others, then certain books have ignored Shakespeare more effectively than others and certain books have undermined the OED more boldly than others.

In terms of the grammatical gravity of obligation, when "have to"'s grossly exceed "want to"'s, "supposed to"'s begin to coerce "willing-to"'s.

A Zen master refers to the wooden plank he uses to spank novices as an "encouragement stick," though some recipients might reword this to "perplexity paddle" or "resentment rod" or "sleeper-swatter."

ⁿⁿ

When "meaning" is a progressive verb it is always at mid-term.
When "meaning" is a static noun it uses a dictionary to stabilize its slant.
When "meaning" is a gerund its noun-ness and verb-ness are at a mental standoff.

Some pages are more aggressively blank than others because they know how to make their whiteness glare like our planet's arctic albedo or a glue-pot grown glassy or a bone-dry clod of baking-soda.

Sometimes carpet static can cause a computer to speak in tongues. Sometimes a half-translated Book of the Dead treats mortality like a sentence fragment. Sometimes a sentence is a space-suit allowing its speaker to travel in zero-gravity semantic conditions.

When a guttural consonant is our grammar undergoing its gag reflex, a liquid consonant is our syntax spooning itself a cough-suppressant.

When the word "tranquil" is reduced to a battery-operated Zen waterfall and the word "kitsch" can't bear to wink at itself, "schlock" gestures to all of its Yiddish kin with an eye-roll and the word "serene" slinks away from its scented candle.

Whether the various conversations at a cocktail party coalesce into a collective C major or B minor depends on the topic of conversation and whether a certain profanity has line-item veto power over the rest of its sentence's other aspirations.

When a word strains but doesn't split
its syllables can display metric sutures at its stress-points
and seam-work where its sense-of-self
sews up its own semantic distress.

For reasons of scale, an observer with a time-frame so vast he could see evolution unfold would look at a library and see a collective comma. For reasons of bulk, a messenger pigeon will always choose a haiku over a history book and a grocery list over a grammar guide.

《±

The scaffolding of a sentence sways every time a semicolon is treated like a screwdriver, an em dash unspools its own measuring-tape, a load-bearing adjective loses its nominal bottom-plate, or a dependent clause leans too heavily on its grammatical support-beams.

A pen is a pricing-gun
when it "marks down" its items into mere inventory:
A pen is a pace-setter
when its affirmative answers can't wait for an interrogative:
A pen is a promotional device
when its print only pertains to its own prowess.

When the buzzing inside of a hypochondriac's ears keeps having its application for additional "z"'s denied, his heart-murmur stocks up on miscellaneous vowels and his elbow-joints and knee-joints learn to syncopate their clicks.

Language's infinite adjective add-on option enables a sentence to telescope outward indefinitely but Language's innermost understatement alternative allows a clause to collapse into a comma.

⹋⹋⹋⹋⹋⹋⹋⹋⹋⹋⹋⹋⹋⹋⹋⹋⹋⹋⹋⹋⹋⹋⹋

Below the Mason-Dixon Line, a dropped terminal consonant and a dropped handkerchief can be equally flirtatious. Above the Mason-Dixon Line, a prolonged vowel and a prolonged stare can be equally pugnacious.

To "de-detail" is to blur together into a single unarticulated mass. To "de-develop" is to allow a storyline to fall back into its non-narrative origins. To "de-demand" is to allow one's insisting to undo itself.

If we have an "etymological unconscious," it is a loamy, rootsy under-region of our mind that is perpetually haunted by the entangled origins of our every utterance. If we have a "letter libido," it understands that the letter "t" most closely resembles a scarecrow propped up on its post because the letter "v" most closely resembles a crow in mid-flight.

A sentence excessive in adjective underbrush can over-accessorize itself out of ensemble-hood and expose its own absence of intellectual acreage.

≽i≽i≽i≽i≽i≽i≽i≽i≽i≽i≽i≽i≽i≽i≽i≽i≽

If our species' initial act of "reading" was our scouring for animal footprints in primeval mud, will our last act of "writing" be our own stumbling, staggering footprints across seas of nuclear ash?

When a Cynic is allowed to have an answer for procedural "How?" as long as she has no answer for motivational "Why?," a Skeptic is allowed to have an answer for a plan-proposing "What?" as long as he has no answer for putting-into-action "When?"

When a surgeon asks a nurse for a particular surgical tool, his one-name "request" and her same-name "response" are a clear demonstration that all nouns have a minimum of two handles.

In certain languages, the words most often shaken, turned upside down, and scattered out across the floor while one looks for a better word tend to develop etymological insecurities.

↓d↓d↓d↓d↓d↓d↓d↓d↓d↓d↓d↓d↓d↓d↓d↓

In most dictionaries, "bestial" is precisely as far away from "nirvana" as "craving" is from "paradise" and "desire" is from "quiescence," even if "erotic" is twice as close to "heavenly" as "profane" is to "venal" and "fallible" is half as far from "illuminated" as "godly" is from "meditative."

Sometimes Slang's satellite burns up upon re-entering "official" English's atmosphere. Sometimes a stammering equivocation is the verbal equivalent of sweeping around a too-heavy-to-move piece of too-tall-to-polish furniture. Sometimes our surface noise needs a core-sampler to examine the meaning-mantle below our conversational crust.

The air trapped inside the closed loops of a lower-case "b" or "d" or "p" form different acoustic micro-climates, depending on the phrasal bioregion and grammatical watershed they are inhabiting.

Sometimes a dictionary is a rear-view magnifying glass sometimes it is a rose-tinted decoder ring and sometimes it is a telescope aimed at a turn in a word's trajectory.

☼<>☼<>☼<>☼<>☼<>☼<>☼<>☼<>☼<>☼<>☼

When a concession speech agrees to play a game called Attorney-Client Privilege Karaoke, a conference call agrees to play Decline-to-Comment Charades and a campaign promise agrees to play Congressional Incumbent Freeze-Tag.

If "run" and "decide" are full-blown verbs, perhaps absences-of-action like "hesitate" and "refuse" should be regarded as "demiverbs" or a "verblets." Even though adjective means "thrown-at," words like "hurled" or "tossed" used as adjectives are no more at home in their function than "handed" or "placed."

If a Profanity Hall of Fame maintained a special wing devoted to a particular four-letter word whose floor was always over-waxed and an observatory devoted to finding obscene angles in the night-sky's constellations, it would also maintain its own wrecking-ball for moments of bitter self-recrimination.

Clothing manufacturers talk about the time "from sketch to rack," while dictionary-makers record the transitions "from slang to cliché" and "from acronym to utterance."

§∞§∞§∞§∞§∞§∞§∞§∞§∞§∞§∞§∞§

When the adjective "early" is an opening act barely allowed to tune up, the noun "arrival" is a headliner with his own dry-ice fog dispenser and laser array.

The wider the bandwidth through which a marriage proposal is broadcast, the more radioactive its rejection, the more maudlin its being misheard, and more hovering its half-acceptance.

The Chinese proverb "No pen can write two words at the same time" hasn't yet caused an argument between the individual bristles of a calligrapher's brush.

Sandpaper feels smooth after petting a porcupine, just as speaking one's own name can feel like a homecoming after failing at a tongue-twister.

⌂∫⌂ ⌂∫⌂ ⌂∫⌂ ⌂∫⌂ ⌂∫⌂ ⌂∫⌂ ⌂∫⌂ ⌂∫⌂

When excavating by means of core-sampling comedy
the fresh humus of our everyday humor
grows out of the rich topsoil of our talking
out of the structural subsoil of our syntax
out of the bedrock of our formative babbling.

Sometimes a micro-aggression is so miniscule it fits inside the innermost lash of an eye-roll. Sometimes a macro-aggression is spelled out in strip-mined canals across a depleted tundra and can only be viewed with a bush-pilot's binoculars.

The vow of silence that uses a system of blinks for consonants and eyebrow-raises for vowels is only "silent" if one believes the non-verbal doesn't have its own sense of "volume." The vow of silence that doesn't survive in slumber knows that some folk merely speak in their sleep while others soliloquize until Stammer and Slur come to a semantic stand-off.

The tautly symmetrical Japanese word for ritual suicide, *hara-kiri* consists of four syllables folded into two internal rhymes, a neat box of verbal closure for an act bent on mortal closure.

If sentences could assemble into the V-shaped flight formations favored by Canadian geese, certain subject-oriented nouns would nose forward to take the lead and certain object-oriented nouns would edge backward to take the tail while transitive verbs absorbed most of the side-draft.

When a speaker too-desperately wants to switch verbal channels halfway through a regretted sentence, the vocabulary equivalent of a remote-control unit is too-often wedged under grammar's sofa-pillows.

People are often a comfortably barefoot native in their first language, a neatly assimilated and naturalized citizen in their second, an easily lost tourist in their third, and a crowbar-wielding trespasser in their fourth.

Sometimes a word's capital letter loses its crown to a lower-case uprising or an idiomatic anti-trust lawsuit. Sometimes a slang term patrols its own streetwise perimeter so that the peace-treaty between its informal vigor and its offensive value can stay balanced.

ⵧⵧⵧ

The Chinese proverb "The closer you look at a word, the more distantly it looks back at you" knows that an unblinking stare can turn the word "banana" into a mantra and the word "discombobulate" into a steeplechase.

The sentence that tries to capture the sense of drowning but contains all of the danger of a video aquarium is related to the sentence that tries to convey the numbness of frostbite but possesses all of the hazard of a hotel mini-fridge.

Update a dictionary on a daily basis and it will pant like a dialect in heat. Update a dictionary on an hourly basis and it will turn into a vernacular blur. Update a dictionary on a yearly basis and it will develop an autumn wardrobe. Update a dictionary every decade and it is in danger of turning into a dogma.

If the word "seduce" skips being used during a seduction because the word "bribe" stays silent during a bribe, sales-staff avoid the word "pitch" because customers cling to the word "catch."

≈∞≈∞≈∞≈∞≈∞≈∞≈∞≈∞≈∞≈∞≈∞≈∞≈∞≈∞≈

One can be "elsewhere" by changing location
    but not "elsewho" by concealing identity
        nor "elsewhat" by altering substance
    nor "elsewhen" by breaking the sound barrier
        nor "elsewhy" by misplacing one's motivations.

If a cybernetically enhanced opera singer is one day able to epically elongate her vowels into century-spanners, an aria will be able to outlive its acoustic end-date, a curtain-call will turn into a calendar-recall, and a Rhinemaiden will ring out past her retirement.

While sleeping, the human body forms into a giant "Y" or "X" or "I" in mid-slumber much easier than a giant "G" or "B" or "Q" for reasons more anatomic than alphabetic and more spinal than semantic.

The most accurate onomatopoeia for the sound of a transitive verb's cue-ball glancing off a direct object's 8-ball would almost certainly not rhyme with "grammar" (or "glancing") and not alliterate with "syntax" (or "sequence.")

《±《±《±《±《±《±《±《±《±《±《±《±《±《±《±《±

The word "ambiguity"'s "at attention" posture and "at ease" posture are as hard to tell apart as the word "ambivalent"'s "urgent care" face and "indifference to suffering" face.

The time it takes for the sincerity-skin of a sentence to snap back after being stretched into a lie is a measure of the suppleness of its syntax. The polysyllabic and Latinate names of certain microbes take longer to pronounce than said organism's fraction-of-a-second lifespan.

The word "and" is a half-second's stutter-step between "signed" and "sealed," a self-aware hesitation between "hemming" and "hawing," a legislative long-jump between "law" and "order," and an agnostic blow to the anatomy between "body" and "soul."

The cooling-off period for accelerating a threat into a promise is about as long as the grace period for backpedaling a warning into an observation.

⁂⁂⁂⁂⁂⁂⁂⁂⁂⁂⁂⁂⁂⁂⁂⁂⁂⁂⁂⁂⁂⁂⁂⁂⁂

Euphemisms are attracted to an obituary
like slanders are to a smear campaign
and smilespeak is to a stewardess seminar.

A period may be the doorstop that prevents the door-slam of an exclamation point, but a comma is the oilcan that lubricates that door's hinges and an ellipsis is the skidmark that memorizes that door's indecisions.

In terms of letter-count, the word "uneven" is no less even than "even" and no more accurate than the odd-lettered non-word "unodd." In terms of letter-count the word "brief" is longer than "long" and exactly as concise as "short."

The ampersands in "Proctor & Gamble" and "Johnson & Johnson" maintain diplomatic relations and the option for a corporate merger while the ampersands in "Rock & Roll" and "Savings & Loan" circle each other warily with their pretzel-like arms crossed in suspicion.

˃á˃á˃á˃á˃á˃á˃á˃á˃á˃á˃á˃á˃á˃á˃á˃

A Bible read through a beekeeper's visor
    blinks its own buzzwords
        and inverts the order of "milk and honey"
            just as a Bible read through a jeweler's lens
                self-adjusts its anti-capitalist jargon
            and abhorrence of overpricing.

The standard newscaster accent plants the occasional California palm tree or New England spruce on the flat, sprawling prairie of its intonation, but tenses its tonsils at the appearance of a Spanish surname's diacritical marks on a teleprompter.

Some nicknames seem designed to half-freeze and half-forgive insults, some to invite further insults and then ambush them, and some to productively mistranslate insults into endearments.

Our interjection-to-adjective
      and our aside-to-explanation ratios
   as well as our alibi-to-asking-pardon
      and our ultimatum-to-apologies ratios
         all tend to rise appreciably
while talking in our grammatically unguarded sleep.

    When classifications are themselves classified, it is by how they categorize the items they contain rather than how they abbreviate the items they exclude.

    A sentence fragment sing-along generally hits its sour notes at its premature periods, its vaulted-over verbs, or its spliced-in-half commas wriggling like amoebae toward an inconclusion.

An unused word that continues to occupy a dictionary isn't the lexical version of an unoccupied investment condo but rather a leftover that has been awarded landmark status.

Carpe diem presses ahead in a jostling crowd of Latin usages better prepared than ad hoc, less self-impressed than bona fide, more self-sustaining than quid pro quo, and less pussy-footed than caveat emptor.

※◇※◇※◇※◇※◇※◇※◇※◇※

The marble dust caused by carving names into tombstones can't be reassembled into a memorial to missing persons by even the most attentive of microscopes.

A brick shaped like an exclamation point is no louder (when dropped) than a brick contoured like a pair of parentheses, whether on the shag carpet of understatement or on the hardwood floor of hyperbole.

The most effective alias is the one that has never even introduced its first name to its middle name. The most effective alibi is the one that hasn't let its escape admit to its reappearance.

> Among the structural adverbs
> "even" is a precisely laid ceiling beam
> and "again" is a repeating support column,
>   "more" is a greedily expansive bay-window
>   and "ever" is a looming clock-tower
>   "always" is an abiding cornerstone
>   and "ago" is a nostalgic back-porch.

§∞§∞§∞§∞§∞§∞§∞§∞§∞§∞§∞§∞§∞

Sometimes an unpaired intransitive verb feels a phantom phonetic ache where its direct object used to be. Sometimes a comma mobilizes upward to become a possessive apostrophe or chromosomally clones itself to enclose a quotation. Sometimes a factoid grows so flagrantly fabricated it forces its footnotes to fade off into futility.

"Less" and "Fewer" race toward a finishing line labeled "None." "Will" and "Shall" arm-wrestle until an auxiliary-verb umpire renders his verdict. "That" and "Which" sow confusion on the furrowed pasture of Clause.

Try to alternate being "exaggeratedly understated" and "humbly hyperbolic" and your adverbs and adjectives will intertwine into oxymorons. Try to issue an "override" command to a half-issued air-kiss and an elbow-bump won't be so eager to serve as an alternate act of endearment.

Taoism refers to lust as "the red thread between the legs" but not to verbosity as "the red thread running up the throat" or to misspelling as "the red thread that tangles and knots itself."

⌂ʃ⌂ ⌂ʃ⌂ ⌂ʃ⌂ ⌂ʃ⌂ ⌂ʃ⌂ ⌂ʃ⌂ ⌂ʃ⌂ ⌂ʃ⌂

Like a chameleon that does chromatic cartwheels when placed on a piece of camouflage cloth, an adjective can alter its intensity depending on the object it is applied to.

The hour-hand and minute-hand on a clock-face can configure into a quarter-past "L" for "Late" or a ten-minutes-till "V" for "Vespertine" or a half-past "I" for "Imminent."

If every genre of literature were written with a stereotypically sharpened animal-bone, epic novels would be written with the antler of a bull-moose, dramedies with the tibia of an exhibitionist ape, and lyric poems with the hollow wing-bone of a skylark.

"E" is the most commonly used letter in English partly because it is the word "English"'s egomaniacal monogram, but "u" is the least used vowel in English despite serving as a homophone for the ego-driven "you."

The surface tension between blank white space and black written letter wouldn't be even vaguely rippled by a book consisting of the word "gray" repeated half a million times. The polarity between a pulp-novel's paper-content and page-layout grows less productive when its plotline begins to perplex even its proofreader.

When an entire sentence can be folded up to fit into a single-syllable outcry, our gut has prevailed over our grammar. When a tattoo is "translated" from old cells into new cells as our skin flakes off, an ink-blot is able to incorporate itself into an age-defying epidermal endurance-test.

Put on your dawn-vision goggles to reduce the glare when reading the Book of Genesis' prologue's foreword's preface and you'll need a particle-sensitive microscope to detect the barely-glowing embers of the Book of Revelation's epilogue's post-script's appendix.

Making good use of one's greetings and goodbyes does not excuse not making good use of one's sentence-centers. Just as some car doors have a more commanding and baritone sense of "slam," some sentence's periods have a firmer and fiercer sense of "finalize."

ⁿⁿ

Et cetera cannot be exaggerated into *ad infinitum*
        unless "unless" agrees to be understated
                out of its incarnation as an ultimatum.

In the dot-dot-dot of an ellipsis, one dot is always trying to jostle itself free from the rank and file and nominate itself as a candidate for a period…

www.ingramcontent.com/pod-product-compliance
Lightning Source LLC
Chambersburg PA
CBHW031635160426
43196CB00006B/432